silly

HAUNTED
HOUSE
JOKES

by Gary Perkins
illustrated by Dan Nevins

Watermill Press

Cover illustration by Maryann Cocca-Leffler

LIBRARY OF CONGRESS CATALOGING-IN-PUBLICATION DATA
Perkins, Gary, (date)
    Silly haunted house jokes / by Gary Perkins; illustrated by Dan
Nevins.
       p.   cm.
    Summary: Riddles feature ghosts, supernatural creatures, and
haunted houses.
    ISBN 0-8167-2963-8 (pbk.)
    1. Wit and humor, Juvenile.   2. Haunted houses—Juvenile humor.
[1. Supernatural—Wit and humor. 2. Riddles. 3. Jokes.]
I. Nevins, Dan, ill.   II. Title.
PN6163.P454   1993
818'.5402—dc20   92-20760

Printed in the United States of America.
10 9 8 7 6 5 4 3 2 1

What room in a haunted house goes flap! flap! flap?

The *bat*room.

What do you call a first-grade monster?

An elementary-ghoul student.

What do ghosts wish on at night?

Mon*stars.*

Where's the best place to build a haunted house?

On a dead-end street.

What did the referee say before the ghost boxing match?

May the best frighter win!

Why was the little ghost crying?

He fell down and got a boo-boo!

What lives in a haunted house and loves the World Series?

A baseball bat.

What do you find on the windows of a haunted house?

Shudders!

What time is it when the clock strikes 13?

Time to get it fixed!

What do you call a skeleton who doesn't like to work?

A lazybones.

What's scarier than the outside of a haunted house?

The inside!

Where do ghosts put up notices?

On a boo-lletin board!

Why do bats go to haunted houses?

Just to hang around.

What do you get if you cross rain clouds with ghosts?

Thunder and frightening.

What does a little vampire call his parents?

Mommy and Batty.

What do you find in the freezer of a haunted house?

Ice scream.

How do you stop baby ghosts from crying?

Change their sheets.

What's scary and rescues ships?

The Ghost Guard.

What is a ghost's favorite dessert?

Boo-berry pie.

What monster tree walks around the forest?

Franken*pine*.

Which member of the ghost hockey team wears a mask?

The ghoulie.

Why is a ghost like a cold breeze?

They both make people shiver.

Why should you never take ghosts to a football game?

They boo every play.

What's wet and spooky?

The Eerie Canal.

What do ghosts put on their salads?

Boo-cheese dressing.

What has wheels and shrieks?

A roller-ghoster.

What does a construction ghost operate?

A *boo*-dozer!

What kind of vampire does somersaults?

An acro*bat*.

Which little monster organization sells cookies?

The Ghoul Scouts.

Where does Dracula brush his teeth?

At the *bat*room sink.

Where are ghost motion pictures made?

In *Howly*wood.

How do ghosts score extra points in football games?

They kick the ball over the ghoul posts.

What do little monsters like to ride at the amusement park?

The scary-go-round.

What game do little ghosts like to play?

Hide and shriek!

Do ghosts take showers?

No. They take boo-ble baths.

What vampire is always eating junk food?

*Snack*ula.

How did the prince feel when the witch turned him into a frog?

He was hopping mad.

What do monsters send in the mail?

*Ghost*cards.

How do you keep a monster from smelling?

Put a clothespin on his nose.

What has big ears and shrieks?

A haunted mouse.

What do monsters like on their mashed potatoes?

Grave-y.

How do you make a sad skeleton laugh?

Tickle its funnybone.

What's ghostly and hops?

A boo-frog!

What time is it when a monster is under your bed?

Time to get up!

What do you call a witch at the beach?

A sand*witch*.

What instrument does a skeleton play?

A trom*bone*.

How do ghosts travel?

By *scare*plane.

What do you call Frankenstein's works of art?

*Monster*pieces.

Where do monsters go when they have a cold?

To a witch doctor.

What do monsters turn on in the summer?

The *scare* conditioner.

What do you put in a vampire flashlight?

Batteries.